PAGES OF LIFE

M HARSHA VARDHAN

Copyright © M Harsha Vardhan
All Rights Reserved.

This book has been published with all efforts taken to make the material error-free after the consent of the author. However, the author and the publisher do not assume and hereby disclaim any liability to any party for any loss, damage, or disruption caused by errors or omissions, whether such errors or omissions result from negligence, accident, or any other cause.

While every effort has been made to avoid any mistake or omission, this publication is being sold on the condition and understanding that neither the author nor the publishers or printers would be liable in any manner to any person by reason of any mistake or omission in this publication or for any action taken or omitted to be taken or advice rendered or accepted on the basis of this work. For any defect in printing or binding the publishers will be liable only to replace the defective copy by another copy of this work then available.

Dedicated to all those who liked expressing their feelings through the art of writing and the ocean of words...

Contents

Contents

Contents

Foreword

Every moment has a story to tell and what if those stories are penned down. Sometimes the unspoken words must be written to prioritise our life. And that life is perfectly reflected in the Pages of Life. Turning back to those pages in this book brings back the lost treasure of core memories.

It's important to have the feminine characteristics in oneself and I felt those while reading them. The most appreciated thing of this book is it just didn't happen within a day but months of work at different situations. Each and every word here showed a lot of emotional weight in them and by the end of the book one can feel to pen down their own emotions.

A million stars in the sky and a million words to speak but one pen to write them down - The Pages of Life

Preface

Pages of Life - is a book that's a collection of my feelings and emotions during some of the best and worst moments of my life. Every word that's in this book was all written during either my happiness or sadness, anger or depression. It's been almost a year and a half since I started writing something, and this book only contains some of those which have been penned by me. My life had been different from the moment I started expressing my emotions and feelings through words. I found myself more calm and I felt more relaxed. Though at times I felt depressed, words and writing made sure I am totally in it. These are the writings that came directly from my heart and made their way into this book, and I hope these bring the smallest of feelings and emotions from your heart.

Acknowledgements

They say writing is a lonely profession and they are wrong. I would like to thank each of those who helped me write and made it to publish.

Kashyap's work has been throughout the book right from the design of the cover page and editing of the content. Making sure we are there on time and making the work easier for me in every aspect.

A big thanks to Sreeja VeeramReddy Garu for her foreword and contribution towards this book. Reading the foreword written by her made me feel that I have developed as a person in writing.

A special mention to Rompalli Harish Garu for the cover page photos that made the book more beautiful than we anticipated.

Parveen has been my constant support at all times irrespective of the situation I am in and her suggestions also helped me express who I am in this book.

Also, I would like to take a moment to thank all my friends who are close to my heart and feel proud to have their blessings during the difficult times.

A special thanks to my father, mother, and sister for making me know what I am, and one special thanks to the #22 batch for everything they did throughout this engineering life...

1. Cricket

Someone asked one day, "Who is it that you love more besides your family?"

I said "cricket" without thinking. They asked, "Why not a person and why cricket?"

I said, "For me, cricket isn't just a game, it's love, which encouraged me in my hard times. It's something that motivated me to do more than my limit." It is the only one that is present in happiness,sadness,in my ups and lows". Cricket isn't just a game; it is something that makes you strive to be the best at the highest pressure. Something that I love, I love even in my anger. And finally, it is not just a game that is apart from my family; it is something that is always included in my heart with my family and my loved ones.

2. Terrace

I was on my terrace, lying on my back, seeing the night sky above me.

It's just not only the stars I am seeing but the moments that made me today. This is what I am feeling. I spent many sleepless nights here contemplating something that happened, is happening, or will happen. When I look up at the sky, my thoughts always return to the times when I cried here for something or laughed here for getting something.
This terrace has always been my go-to place, not just for seeing the night sky but also for controlling my feelings. Seeing the stars always makes me happy, not just from the outside but from the inside of my heart. Seeing the moon makes me feel lighter and my heart will dance with happiness. All these years have been a roller coaster ride for life with its ups and downs, and never have I felt bored lying on the terrace and watching the night.

My childhood wouldn't have been complete without watching those twinkling stars and shining moon. My memories are incomplete without my mom feeding me the food here and saying the stories of the moon and the stars. My life is nothing without those wonderful words my father would say while lying on the terrace. My knowledge is incomplete without hearing my grandfather's life experience.

Nothing is enough to write about this place here on the terrace, but my feelings for this place and love will always double with each passing day...

3. A Beautiful Dream

One day, I was sitting all alone by myself, just doing nothing and watching the moon from my window at midnight, and then I heard someone calling me, so I turned around to see who it was and found no one there. So I just started watching the moon again. Then again, I heard someone calling me in the sweetest voice that I have ever heard, so again I turned around and found no one, and this time I saw all around the place, but there's just no one and there's nothing that's making any sound. After a while, I again heard my name, but this time not just from the back but from all around me. When someone called me, I heard my name in the sweetest way possible. Then came the voice that melted my heart. Then came the words that made me smile. Then came the music that made me dance, and then came the thoughts that made me crazy. The voice stayed with me till the night disappeared. The music reverberated till the morning, and the dance continued till the dream disappeared.

4. She's The Star

The night has been glorious, with the moon shining bright and the stars twinkling, and the scene has been a delight for my eyes as they see the infinite beauty of the night sky. I was there by myself, doing nothing but the most difficult thing in life: enjoying the sights of nature. As I saw the night sky, my thoughts travelled back to the most memorable days I ever had. I saw the successes that kept me on top and the failures that burried me down. I saw the smile and I saw the tears and then suddenly came a person who sat by me and started talking all about me like she knew me better than I did. The more she talked, the more I felt comfortable. The more she smiled, looking at me, the more pleasure I felt inside. The more she looked at me, the more my eyes glued to her, and then when I started talking to her, I observed that my words were stopped in my mouth, but she still smiled like she heard what I was about to say, and then she disappeared suddenly in the night sky from where she came from, and then I saw a star twinkle more brightly than ever before, and I thought maybe she must be the star who came to give company to the friend who's alone. Maybe she's the star who came to say that she's for me, and maybe she's the star who will twinkle every time I smile while looking at the night sky.

5. Sun Rise

Early in the morning, with time past 4, I was sitting along the beach waiting for the sun to rise. As I started to see those first rays of the sun light, my eyes fixed in the direction of sunrise to absorb the whole amount of heat that was coming out. My body started to feel the pleasure of the sun's rays as they touched every cell in my body. As the sun was on the horizon, I stood tall to enjoy every bit of heat. As the sun totally went down in the sky, I sat on the beach with the waves of the sea touching my feet. Every time the waves touched my feet, I had a divine feeling that just melted my heart. Every time I see the waves rising in the distance, my eyes are fixed to see how it's going to end. Every time the wave ended, I saw a new wave rise in the distance. As the sand below me started to heat up, my body felt the urge to go into the sea and enjoy, but every time I thought to go, my heart stopped me to enjoy the silence that comes after every wave ends and to enjoy the waves hitting the beach far in the distance from where I sat. I continued to sit there till the sun set and the night started to take its place, but never once did I feel an inch of boredom taking over me...

6. Infinite Thoughts

It's been late at night and the thoughts in my mind have not allowed me to sleep. So I was just awake and thinking about them. Just when I started to know them, along came the new thoughts that just blew my mind. My body was tired of it, and it's hard to be awake when the heart and the mind are just playing with my body. The moment I found the meaning of the thoughts, new ones arrived, and then again they repeated the same. Then came a cool breeze, which simply took away all those unwanted thoughts and brought silence to my mind, as well as the unwanted feelings in my heart, which simply brought peace to it. The cool breeze brought the best music for my ears to hear and the best memories for my eyes to see. It gave me the best smile I could ever have and the best sleep I could ever get.

7. Beautiful Evening

It was half past five in the evening, and I was sitting on the hilltop facing the sun. As the sun started to set, the view became more amazing with each passing second. The clouds around the setting sun added that extra beauty, which made my eyes blink less. As the sun touched the horizon, I saw the lights from the top of the hills in the villages just starting to turn on. As the sun disappeared, the view of lights filled my heart to the fullest. As I see the villages, which are separated by the distance, the lights from each village radiate like its own type. I saw the beauty in the darkness and the addition of light to it. As I started to get down the hill, my mind just couldn't help me get away from the beautiful views that my eyes saw. In every step of mine, I could see the beauty that the evening and night gave me. In every breath I took, I saw the beauty of the sunset and the darkness. Every second I spent was like a lifetime experience, and every time I remember it, I am just mesmerised by the beauty of nature.

8. Rain Is Love

It's 4 in the evening and the clouds are pouring down rain as if it hasn't rained for years. A part of me thought it was the perfect time to hang out. So I just changed into my nightwear and started to walk in the rain. I saw people observing me like an idiot. I saw my fellow friends laughing at me because of my behavior, but my mind and heart cared very little about them all, as they were in a hurry to enjoy nature with the black clouds above, the rain drops in the middle, and the water everywhere on the ground. I walked a bit and sat on a bench in the rain. As the raindrops flowed through my body, I felt the pleasure that nothing gives. As the raindrops fell on my body, I felt like this is what heaven is made of. As the clouds continued to pour down rain on the ground, I felt a sharp pain in my heart which just started to make me cry. I cried there alone in the rain, just making sure that no one could see what I was going through.

I cried there alone till the last bit of water in my eyes dried up. I cried there alone, making sure that I didn't cry for the same reason again. I cried there alone because I just wanted to make sure that the tears couldn't be seen with the rain. I made sure it was just the normal water. But I know what the raindrops are mixed with as they flow through my cheeks. The rain knew the pain I had. The rain knew how I was suffering, and the rain was the only one that knew I cried there. As the tears in my eyes dried up, I looked back at the pouring clouds and said a big thanks to them for making me feel lighter, and then I started to walk back to my room, but this time with my heart feeling light and my mind finding peace in the rain.

9. A Great Time Pass

These days, when I start to write something, my mind just can't get the idea of what to write. If something struck my mind and I started to write about it, the thoughts in my mind would disappear as if they never appeared. I would just think of what I wanted to write for hours with my blank mind. Maybe I was never born to write or express myself. Maybe I was never born to showcase what I feel in words. Maybe those which I have written were just a laughing piece to all the others. Maybe my words were just a set of comedies that everyone could laugh at and comment on. Maybe I never had the capacity to write something and make someone feel better about it. Maybe I shouldn't have started writing and expressing myself, but I still write something to just pass my time...

10. I Am Hard and Tough

I was in bed thinking about sleeping. I was exhausted from the day's work and every cell in my body wanted a tight sleep. The headache is unbearable and my own brain is giving up on everything. As I was typing, my hands felt numb and my legs were like those that were under a lot of loads. My eyelids just couldn't hang on and they seemed to close at the very right moment. But something inside of me is pushing me to let my feelings be expressed, not to people, but to words. As I type this, I felt my own eyes burning like a volcano, and the heat inside was coming out like an eruption, but still, I don't know how I managed everything. Maybe I still have a little bit of control over my body. Maybe my body felt the need to express my pain through these words and to those who are reading this. With each passing second, I feel like death might overtake me, but I still hope to live, not just to live but to show that I can withstand whatever the situation is. I will live to show them that my unbearable pain will never let me make any hasty decisions and I will live to show how hard and tough I am...

11. Write and Rewrite

Sometimes I write and rewrite the same things many times. I don't know what forces me to do it, but still, every time I write about it, I feel like I'm writing about it for the first time. Sometimes my lack of thought makes me write about the same things repeatedly. Sometimes my lack of ideas makes me write about the same things over and over. Sometimes my lack of words makes me write about the same things. But I never felt bored with writing about the same things. Maybe you have felt bored reading it, but I cared less because I write to express what I feel through those beautiful words that keep me alive...

12. Scars

Scars are what make a warrior really proud, and I am no different from that. My scars might not appear on my body, but my heart now knows the depth of the scars I had. I feel proud of having them because those scars are what showed me the difference between the fake and the real. Those scars are what made me who I am today, and they are the ones that make me new every day. Scars are good, and being afraid of them makes you feel bored...

13. A Bit Of Me

A bit of me wants to die, while a bit of me wants to live. A bit of me wants to cry, while a bit of me wants to laugh. A bit of me wants to be with someone, while a bit of me wants to be alone. A bit of me wants hell, while a bit of me wants heaven. A bit of me wants to work, while a bit of me wants the rest. A bit of me felt bored, while a bit of me felt curious. A bit of me felt happy, while a bit of me felt sad. A bit of me is angry, while a bit of me wants pleasure. A bit of me wants to be recognized, while a bit of me wants to be ignored. A bit of me needed friends, while a bit of me needed a family. A bit of me needed you, while a bit of me never wanted to leave you...

14. Far Ahead

Far ahead, I can see the darkest days that will be my companion. I can see the worst that can hit me hard and I can see the slightest mistakes that make me feel bad, but still, with all these things, I still see the best of me handling them with better perfection every time they hit me. I can see those darkest days making me a tougher person who will regret being with me. I can see myself still smiling with them and my heart pounding out loud that I can still be the best with all of them.

15. My Own People

For every drop of tear I shed, I know the pain behind it. For every hint of a smile I had, I knew the reason behind it. For every second of my sadness, I know the feeling behind it. For every bit of happiness, I know the people behind it. When I look back to when I was young, I remember the tough times I had. I remember the reasons for them. I remember the pain I had then. I remember the happiness I had. I remember the sadness I went through and the tears I shed. But seeing those, I just don't see my feelings, but I see the ones who stood by me and who left me. I feel proud to have those who stood by me in those tough times. I was ashamed of myself when someone I trusted abandoned me during a difficult time. Although time heals all wounds, the people who loved you will heal your past and build your future. It's this that I dedicate to all those who know what they are when they read it.

16. A Girl

Late in the night, I started crying for reasons which I couldn't figure out. I cried and cried until the tears in my eyes dried up. Then came a girl who sat beside me and placed her hand around my shoulder. Neither of us talked. The silence ruled the time when we were together. The more she looked into my eyes, the stronger I became. The more she smiled at me, the bigger my smile grew, but the silence was still there. I don't know who she is and don't know how she came, but all that mattered to me was that she came. She came for her friend, whom she always wanted to stand by and show him that she would be there for him always.

17. The Sharp Pain

Every night as I go to sleep, there comes a sharp pain in my left leg just below the knee. I don't know if it would be there all the time or just come when I needed to sleep or play cricket, but it comes. The pain would be like having knives driven through the leg and then taken back. I spent nights wondering why this was happening to me, and I cursed myself for putting myself through such agony. But eventually, I got through it. I go through it each night while sleeping and in my sleep. It's fucking hard to bear, but still, I just couldn't find a way to stop. There were times when I just wanted to cut my leg off and live, but I still hope that someday the pain will stop suddenly like how it has come. The pain makes me go through hell every day and night and the reason and the solution to it are still unknown.

18. A Tide In The Ocean

Once, there was a tide in an ocean that was feared for its fall. While the other tides of the ocean enjoy the beauty of rising and falling tides, this tide is feared for the fall. The tide wanted to stay still and never wanted any ups or downs. As time went by, the tide tired of being still. So it started its journey. Though the tide was feared, it was never feared to rise high. On our journey to the beach, the tide first rose so high that it's never been, and then it started to fall. The tide was feared, but still, it's been able to complete the fall. Then again, it started to rise again, and again it fell into the ocean. After 2-3 times, it no longer felt like a fear of falling. From then on, it never feared falling. Because it knew that it would rise again after every fall, and it would fall after every rise...

19. Unknown Words

• 21 •

Numerous thoughts reverberated through my mind. The emotions of the thoughts aren't just one, and the words that I have to express them are so few that I find myself thinking about every word. I find myself illiterate in the process of expressing my thoughts and I find myself useless in the process of showing emotions. Every day and every night, every minute and every second, the thoughts were full in my mind. But for every thought, there aren't any words that express how I feel. I'm still looking for words to express my feelings the way I want to...

20. You

Every time I feel happy or depressed, I open the old chats of us, to read, to stop my anxiety or depression that's taking over me. I see your picture every time I feel low, so you know I can stand and run for you. I see your eyes when the whole world is sleeping. I remember the times we spent together alone when I was alone and had nothing to do. But I've never stopped falling for you. Either your looks or your smile, either your thoughts or your words, everything makes me smile and laugh until the thought of you disappears.

21. The Words

The words that come from these thoughts are the ones that make your heart feel light. The words that emerge from your silence express your feelings, while the words that emerge from the heart express love. Every time I feel alone, I fall silent and my thoughts race to find the perfect words to express myself, and every time I fall for someone or something, I hear the words coming from the heart that have pure feelings in them...

22. The Waves

The waves in the ocean sometimes represent the waves of emotions in me. When I feel calm and cool, I feel the waves are the coolest things that start their journey in the sea and end up at the beach. When I feel sad and depressed, I see the waves falling every time. When I require a bit of motivation, I see how the waves rise after every fall. When I am angry, I see the force with which the waves attack the things that come into contact with them. When I feel happy, I see the waves rising and moving as if they are meant to be...

23. For A Better Version

When I find myself in some of my darkest days, I reflect on how I spent them at the time.I know they are the worst aspects of myself, but I am proud of how I spent those days.I feel happy about sharing those darkest days because they are what made me what I am today. Those darkest days made me realise how I am, and those darkest days showed me a way to become a better version of myself...

24. Scream

When there's a lot of shit going through my mind, I will just be myself alone and scream out aloud till the frustration in me all gets over and out. I scream out till the last bit of my energy in me dies out. I scream out till the nerves in my throat get the pain, and I scream out to make sure that I don't experience the same pain again.

25. Worst Memories and Best Lessons

Some days are so dark that remembering them makes us so emotional that we just can't hold back our emotions. Those days are like a black spot that shows how irresponsible and unthoughtful you are. Remembering those days sometimes makes us so weak that we just can't help ourselves and the tears in our eyes can't be held back. Those days are the worst memories we can ever have, and they teach us the best lessons that we can never learn.

26. A Magical Coffee

Millions of thoughts are racing through my mind and each one has its impact on me and makes me feel depressed. Each thought struck my heart like a needle, making me feel the pain that was unbearable. I know the pain is unnecessary and the thoughts useless, yet my mind can't resist having them. Just as the thoughts started to make me angry, I had my first sip of coffee. The caffeine hit me hard, making my thoughts disappear. I know they will come back, but still, the pleasure after having the coffee and the caffeine having its impact on my painful thoughts made me quiet. After the last sip of my coffee, I smiled at myself and continued to do my work.

27. Depression

When your heart's full of depression and feelings a second feels like an hour and the anxiety in you kills you every second. The time moves slow and everything you see looks like it's going to kill you emotionally and mentally. You feel like The people you loved the most are ignoring you and the ones who need to stand by you will never look at you and it hurts a lot...

28. New Me

As the days passed, I saw a new me evolving. I saw a new me in every aspect of my life. I was amazed at how the new me controlled my anger. I was taken aback by how well the new me handled things. I was astonished at the way the new me found happiness in small things. People seeing the new me said many things about me, but the new me just smiled at them and started to enjoy my own company. I saw the new me finding new things, and I wanted the new me to be who I am and to love what I am irrespective of what's happening around me.

29. Unknown Pain

I don't know what made me write this, and I don't know the meaning of what I am writing. But my thoughts insisted on me writing this. Either the lack of sleep from the last few days or the ignorance of my favourite people and also maybe, the wildest pain in my heart, might have made me write this. The pain played a serious role in my heart in writing this, but the reason for the pain is unknown. The feelings for the one I loved the most might have made me write this, but the reason for the feelings is unknown. The people I loved the most might be the ones writing this, but the reason is unknown.

30. A day For Myself

For a long time, today has been the day that I always wanted it to be. I did what I liked the most, travelled where I liked the most and enjoyed the way I wanted. A day that had everything in it that I could ask for on a given day. I ate the food I desired, drank the coffee I desired, and sat by the beach as I frequently do. I drove the bike to all the places that I wanted to see and enjoyed the views that I could see. A day for myself A day I'd been looking forward to for a long time and the one I'll remember until my last breath...

31. Pleasure

The evening had been cool, and suddenly it started to rain. I was sitting on the balcony enjoying the cold just before the rain. As soon as it started raining, I made my way quickly into the kitchen and made myself a strong coffee. I could hear the sounds of the raindrops falling on the trees and I could hear the sounds of the rain falling on the earth. I poured my coffee into a cup and went back to the balcony. I sat on a chair on the balcony and began to sip my hot coffee while watching the rain fall. With each sip of hot coffee and each drop of cool rainwater falling on me, I felt the pleasure running through my nerves and into my heart...

32. The Questions

As time passing, there were a lot of questions kept raised in my mind. The questions that made me curious and the questions that kept me interested in someone or something. The questions that made me confused and the ones that made me anxious The questions that arise in me are the reason for the anger I possess, and sometimes they are the reason for the peace I have. The questions that raised are the reasons for my happiness and my sadness, but still, they are the reason why I am living. Those are the things that keep me alive. Waiting for the answers to all those questions to be revealed with time...

33. Terrace and The Girl

Lying on the terrace, feeling the breeze on my face and hearing the songs, it felt like someone was sitting by my side. I felt like someone was holding my hand and patting me on the back. I can hear her smile and I can smell her scent. I can sense her around me, lying by my side. My thoughts stopped as soon as I sensed her. My feelings halted as soon as I felt her. I can't see her, but I can sense every bit of her. I don't know who she is, but I know where she's from. She has come from my thoughts and my loneliness. She has come from my heart and from my feelings.

34. My Silence

My silence had an infinite number of questions in it. My most aggressive nature was reflected in my silence. My silence of mine had the deepest expression of sorrow unexpressed. My silence shed the heaviest of tears from my eyes. My silence felt the ignorance of many. The silence of mine wanted the fucking shit to end here and the silence of mine sometimes wanted my life to end, My silence wanted me to die at times, and my silence wanted me to be who I am forever...

35. I Cried

I don't know what happened and I don't know what made it happen, but tears started to roll down my cheeks. The reason for the tears is unknown, like many of my feelings. Either it's the loneliness or the ignorance of people that made me cry. Either it's the unshown anger or it's the unexpressed feelings that made me cry. Either it's the useless me or the useless thoughts that made me cry. But I cried unknowingly till the tears in my eyes dried and the eyes became sore and red. I cried.

36. About You

The class felt bored and the time kept slowing down. The surroundings around me started to make me irritated and angry. It was just the moment I saw you. My eyes stared at you for the first time ever. Looking at your eyes, my eyes found the spark they needed. When you're around, time seems to fly by. Your voice felt like music, and you looked like an angel who came from heaven. My eyes paused at your sight, and my ears concentrated on your words. My thoughts never ended and my feelings never stopped...

37. Someone

Sitting in a garden, surrounded by nature, I found heaven on earth. My eyes were drawn to the never-ending mountains of lush green trees, with clouds covering the entire sky, creating a romantic atmosphere. Hearing the chirping of the birds and feeling the breeze on my face, I felt like being somewhere in Heavan. My heart urged me to find someone who could sit with me and talk to me. My heart urged me to find someone who could make me laugh. My heart yearned for someone who could make me love, someone who could understand my thoughts, someone who would be there for me in my lowest lows, and someone who could make me live as I am...

38. My Love

It's been a long time since I saw you. As the time went by from the last time I saw you, every cell in my body wanted to see you. Then came a day, after many years, when the eyes of mine could look at your eyes for the first time in a while. Then came a day when the ears of mine could hear the magical words of yours. The moment my eyes found you, tears started rolling down my cheeks. I wanted to hide them, but the love I had for you made me cry. I know you won't look back at me or talk to me, but the moment I saw you, it's been like a dream come true. Seeing you brought back the wonderful memories I had with you, not in person but in my thoughts. Seeing you brought back the old me and it brought back the painful times. But still, seeing you now just made me who I am, and seeing made me be who I am...

39. I Love You

I saw her walking towards me from a distance. She had a rose and a letter in her hand, holding them back. As the distance between her and me reduced, my heartbeat started to rise. She came right in front of me and stopped. She has been the love I have been waiting for all these days. The memories and the moments we had are all that makes me now. She bent to her knees and looked into my eyes. With the deepest of her looks, she said those three magical words, "I LOVE YOU." I couldn't resist the tears in my eyes. The tears started to flow down my cheeks with the utmost happiness. It was like a dream come true, and I kissed and hugged her until we promised to stay and fight for each other until our bodies were buried.

40. The Best Time

It's not every day you get to talk to your best friend for hours, though you are nearby, and today has been such a kind of a day where we had that time for ourselves. To talk about the random things that are happening around us and in our lives and to laugh at those funny things that happen during the course of time. Hours passed but the words between us never stopped, as they seemed to flow like a river. It's been one of those days when at the end I felt like I had had one of the best times of my life...

41. Searching For Words

It's been almost a week since I wrote something and it's the longest gap between the time I started writing something. The feelings have been high all this week with myself wanting to write something but still, I either couldn't find time or words to write. Even now my mind just couldn't find words and for the 1st time ever I have been searching for more words to express more of my feelings whether they are happy one's or sad one's...

42. A Stranger

It's not every day I talk to a stranger and become friends. Also, it's not every day a stranger asks you to talk as it's boring. The shyness in me disappeared as soon as we started talking and we talked like the ones who knew each other for years. We talked about everything we could as the ones who met first and also everything we could as people who had known each other for a long time. And I would confess that the time I spent with her throughout the whole journey will be remembered and cherished, for it's such a moment that happens very rarely in one's life.

43. The Best Days

•

Those last few days of my life have been some of the best days I've ever lived. Travelling to different places and staying there is a whole new and different experience, and that, along with some of the best buddies of engineering life, made the trip even more fun. Starting the trip with cooking food with the seniors and having it with them and then starting the journey was one of the best starts we got for the trip. Every aspect of the trip has just been what we wanted, and there were times when our expectations were crossed. The memories we made throughout the whole journey will always have a special place in my heart, and the fun we had will always be cherished.

44. An Eventful Life

The last 3-4 months of my college life has has been one of the best times I had ever. That period had some of the finest memories one can make in his engineering life. We have had trips, We have had games, we have had department day and all in all we had our freshers, food party. It was during this period we had the best funny conversations with our seniors and with our classmates. It's during this period we just planned a trip a day before and completed it and it's during this period I had the best time with people whom I loved and cared about...

45. Coffee and Heavan

• 47 •

The wind has been strong and the sky has been thundering, making it a perfect set-up. I just made myself a hot cup of coffee and made my way to the terrace. Sitting on the terrace and feeling the strong wind and seeing the lightning sky, I started to sip the coffee, soaking at the moment. It's like being in Heaven and then I felt like writing something just to make the moment more memorable and, seriously, after a boring week, this certainly is the best time I had...

46. We

I was sleeping when I woke suddenly to a dream that disturbed my sleep. I saw a girl coming towards me with a bunch of flowers and a letter. I saw the spark in her eyes as she was approaching me. I saw the smile as she saw me and I saw the cuteness on her face as she giggled. Looking into my eyes, she spoke her heart, expressing her feelings and me listened. During all this, tears flowed down my cheeks, and we just hugged, expressing our feelings just when the dream was shattered, never to come again.

47. Shades Of People

I saw people change right in front of my eyes. I saw them moving away from me and, as days passed, I came to know what I was to them. It's been difficult to accept it at first, but as time flew by, I found it comfortable. I never feared losing people anymore because I knew how they treated me and how much I respected them.

48. Why I Write

People ask me why I always write something and I say nothing to them because it's something I feel that they can never understand and I smile at them.

Then one day I asked myself why I write so much and this time my heart replied, " You write to show how angry you are at times. You write to show how happy you are at times. You write to show how peaceful you are. You write to show how emotional you are. You write to show how good you are at times. You write to show how bad you are. You write to show how anxious you are. You write to show how strong you are. You write to show how weak you are. You write to show the physical and mental pain you experience. "You write to show how much you love a person and you write to show what a person cannot express." Hearing this from within me, my eyes shed tears not of sadness or happiness but of something that I found in between the two...

49. Dad

I saw some of the best moments through my eyes. I saw something near-impossible become possible, and all this time, I would look at the people who accomplished those great things. They are a hero whether they are on the winning or losing side. And for me, one of my biggest heroes is my dad. When I felt I was short, he would make me sit on his shoulders and show me the world. When I was disturbed and done, he would make me feel comfortable. When I was anxious and depressed, he would hug me tight to say that he was there for me. When I am happy, he will smile every time I look at him. When I made mistakes, he never saw the intent behind my actions; all he wanted me to know was why they were wrong. When the world stood against me, he fought for me, and when I conquered the world, he led me to the throne. When I wanted stories, he became a storyteller, and when I was curious, he became my teacher. When I was alone, he became my best friend, and when I was leaving him, he became a path. When I was bored, he became an entertainer, and when I wanted energy, he became my inspiration.

50. A Dream

Like everyone, I once dreamed of having my name on a cover page as an author. I never thought that it would come true, and when I started writing a book, I never thought I would publish it. When I sent the book for review, I never thought that it would be selected for publishing. Then when it was published, I felt all this was a dream and when I got the 1st book with my name on the cover page, I knew I had achieved something. I know it's just a book that's been published, but when it happened and I saw my name as an author, I felt emotional and cried. I cried feeling proud of myself, and I cried knowing that I am something rather than nothing.